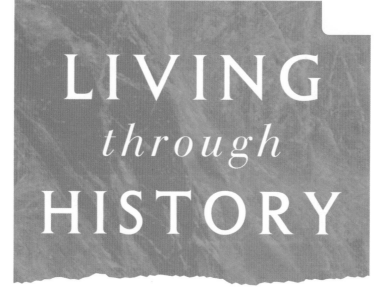

LIVING *through* HISTORY

Foundation Edition

the Roman Empire

Fiona Reynoldson
and
David Taylor

Heinemann

Acknowledgements

The authors and publishers would like to thank the following for permission to reproduce photographs:

Ancient Art & Architecture Collection: 1.1A, 1.1B, 5.1C, 8.1B
Bridgeman Art Library/Tabley House, University of Manchester: 5.1A
British Museum: 1.2B, p52, 6.5A, 6.6C
Brookside Productions: 1.4A
University of Cambridge/Aerial photography collection: 7.2B
Colchester Museums: 3.1D
C.M. Dixon: 2.1A, 3.3B, 6.6A
Robert Estall Photo Library/Malcolm Aird: 7.3D
Michael Holford: 4.1A, 4.1B
A K Kersting: 8.1A
Kobal Collection/MGM: 6.2A
Rex Features: 1.4B
Scala/Galleria Borghese, Rome: 6.2C
Scala/Museo della Ciuilta Romana, Rome: 6.1B
Society of Antiquaries of London: 3.2A
Edwin Smith: 5.1E
The National Trust Photographic Library/ Ian Shaw: 6.4B
Werner Forman Archive: 5.1C
York Archaeological Trust: 1.4A

The publishers have made every effort to trace copyright holders of material in this book. Any omissions will be rectified in subsequent printings if notice is given to the publisher.

The authors and publishers gratefully acknowledge the following publications from which written sources in the book are drawn. In some sources the wording or sentence structure has been simplified.

A Bowman, *Life and Letters on the Roman Frontier*, British Museum Press, 1994: 3.3C, 7.5F
Julius Caesar, *The Conquest of Gaul*, trans. S A Handford, Penguin, 1982: 7.1B
F R Conwell, *Everyday Life in Ancient Rome*, B T Batsford, 1963: 6.4D
Cassius Dio, *Roman History*, trans. E Cary, Harvard UP, 1925: 7.3A
C Greig, Pliny: *A Selection of his Letters*, CUP, 1978: 5.1B, 6.2B
The *Guardian*, 16th January, 1997: 6.5B
Josephus, *The Jewish War*, ed. E M Smallwood, Penguin, 1981: 3.1C
Livy, *The Early History of Rome*, trans. A De Selincourt, Penguin, 1969: 2.2A
R D MacNaughten (trans.), *Rome, its People, Life and Customs*, McKay, 1963: 6.1C
Martial, *The Twelve Books of Epigrams*, trans. J A Pott and F A Wright, Dutton, 1924: 6.4E
R Nichols and K McLeith, *Through Roman Eyes*, OUP, 1976: 6.2D, 6.6B
QED – The Body in the Bog, BBC Television, 1985: 1.2D, 1.2E
The Sunday Times magazine, 6th April, 1997: 1.2C
Gaius Suetonius Tranquillus, *The Twelve Caesars*, trans. R Graves, The Folio Society, 1957: 1.1C
Tacitus, *The Imperial Annals of Rome*, trans. M Grant, Penguin, 1973: 3.1A, 7.2A, 77.3E,. 7.3F
The Times, 26th September, 1996: 3.3C
J Wilkes, *The Roman Army*, CUP, 1972: 3.3A

Reed Educational and Professional Publishing Ltd
Halley Court, Jordan Hill, Oxford OX2 8EJ

MELBOURNE AUCKLAND FLORENCE PRAGUE
MADRID ATHENS SINGAPORE TOKYO
SAO PAULO CHICAGO PORTSMOUTH NH
MEXICO IBADAN GABORONE JOHANNESBURG
KAMPALA NAIROBI

© Fiona Reynoldson and David Taylor 1997

The moral rights of the proprietors have been asserted.

First published 1997

00 99 98 97
10 9 8 7 6 5 4 3 2 1

British Library Cataloguing in Publication Data is available from the British Library on request.

ISBN 0435 309 579

Designed and produced by Dennis Fairey and Associates Ltd

Illustrated by Richard Berridge, Finbarr O' Connor, John James, Angus McBride, Arthur Phillips, Piers Sanford and Stephen Wisdom.

Printed in Hong Kong by Wing King Tong Co. Ltd.

Cover design by Wooden Ark

Cover photograph: *Ministrant Carrying a Tray of Food with Silenus Playing a Lyre and a young Satyr Playing a Syrinx*, North Wall, Oecuss, 60–50 BC, Courtesy of Villa dei Misteri, Pompeii/Bridgeman Art Library, London.

CONTENTS

The Romans lived hundreds of years ago. It is hard to find out about people who lived such a long time ago. There are two ways of finding out about the Romans.

1 Finding out from archaeology

Many things from Roman times have been covered by soil. **Archaeologists** dig up the ground to look for old things.

Archaelologists look for a good place to dig.

Lots of broken Roman pottery in this field.

What a find!

They could find the ruins of a Roman villa and lots of coins, jewellery etc.

Source A

Many Roman buildings were huge and have not fallen down. This shows how good the Romans were at building. The Romans built this stadium called the Colosseum. A lot of it is still standing.

Roman writing on stone found on Hadrian's Wall. It says that the Roman army built that part of the Wall.

Source B

2 Finding out from Roman writing

a Writing on stone: We have found Roman carving and writing on stones. One soldier even carved rude names about the emperor on a wall. It was a good job that he was not found out!

b Books: We still have some books which were written by the Romans. They tell us a lot about how the Romans lived. The Romans wrote in Latin. So we have to translate what they wrote.

Source C

This Roman is writing about the Emperor Nero. Nero was dead when it was written, otherwise it would not have been so nasty.

At night he walks the streets looking for trouble. He used to stab men on their way home from dinner.

Nero also went shoplifting. Afterwards he set up a market stall to sell the goods he had stolen!

Source D

Archaeologists often find things which the Romans used every day. These are Roman sandals.

Questions

1 Read **Finding out from archaeology**.
   What do archaeologists do?

2 Read **Finding out from Roman writing**.

   a Which two kinds of writing have the Romans left us?
   b What language did the Romans use?

3 Look at Source A.

   a What was the Colosseum?
   b Why is a lot of it still standing?

4 Read Source C.
   Why did the writer of this source dare to be nasty about Nero?

Good fun!

Archaeologists do not just dig up things from the ground.

They also try to guess what these things were, and what they tell us about people in the past.

This is the fun part of their job.

Sometimes archaeologists find some very interesting things! (Look at Source A.)

Source A

Archaeologists often find some unusual things. This is a piece of human faeces, which is over a thousand years old! Archaeologists dug it up in York.

From looking at it, scientists can tell that the person had eaten a kind of bran and also had worms!

Lindow man

In 1984 workmen found a body in a peat bog at Lindow Moss, near Manchester.

The body was in very good condition. How long had it been in the bog?

Scientists carried out tests on the body. They said that the body had been in the bog since 500 BC!

The acid in the peat had kept the body in good condition. The scientists called the body Lindow man. (The workmen who found the body had called it Pete Marsh!)

Questions and more questions

Who was this man? What had happened to him? Why did he die? How did he die?

Scientists carried out some more tests to see if they could answer these questions.

What the tests showed

1 Lindow man had smooth finger nails. He might have made cloth. This would have smoothed his nails.

2 Fox hairs were found on his body. Perhaps he was wearing a fox fur to keep warm.

3 Bran and burnt wheat grains were found in Lindow man's stomach. He must have eaten a kind of bread just before he died.

4 Worms were also found in his stomach!

Question

Read Sources C and E on page 7. Why might Lindow man have been killed?

A nasty end!

The scientists found a rope around Lindow man's neck. He had probably been strangled. The body had some cuts on it as well.

It looks like Lindow man met a horrible death.

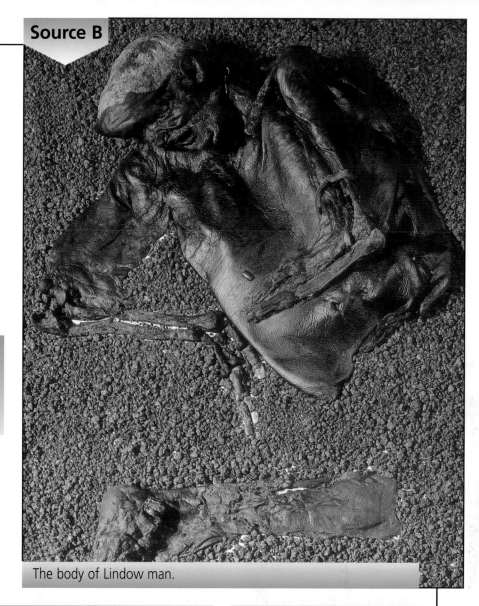

The body of Lindow man.

Source C

From a magazine article, 6 April 1997.

Lindow man had mistletoe juice in his stomach. We know that mistletoe was used when offerings were made to please a god. Lindow man could have been killed as a sacrifice to a god.

Source D

What a modern scientist says about the death of Lindow man.

He was knocked out so he could not fight back.

There is a wound in his head. It looks as if he was hit with an axe.

The rope cut into his neck. His neck was broken.

There is also a cut about two inches long over the jugular vein in the neck.

Source E

A historian's view about why Lindow man died.

He was completely naked. I think he was part of a sacrifice to a god. The area around Manchester is cold. He would not have been walking about naked out of choice!

1.3 CAN YOU ALWAYS TRUST HISTORICAL SOURCES?

Sources

Sources are things which tells us about the past. They give us clues or evidence. There are many different types of sources.

Problems with written sources

You cannot always trust what written sources say. They might not be telling the truth. Why is this?

1 The writer may not have known the exact truth.

2 The writer might be **biased** and only giving one side of the story.

Read the two newspaper reports on page 9. They are both reporting the same football match, but they each describe the match from their side only.

Newspaper A

SUPER NEWCHESTER BEAT MANHAMPTON

Newchester 3 Manhampton 2

Newchester played brilliant football on Saturday.

They never stopped attacking the Manhampton goal and could have been several goals in the lead by half time.

In the second half Newchester were given two penalties. Dave Smith scored easily from both. The goalkeeper had no chance.

The Newchester forwards were much too fast for Manhampton. In the final minute, Jones headed the ball into his own goal to give Newchester a great win by 3–2.

Questions

1 Read **Newspaper A** and **Newspaper B**.

  a Which newspaper was printed in Newchester?
  b Which newspaper was printed in Manhampton?
  c How did you tell?

2 Why should we be careful when using written historical sources?

Be careful

A lot of the written sources in this book are by Romans.

Some of them might be telling the truth. But if they keep saying the Romans are great, they might be giving only one side of the story.

So take care!

Newspaper B

BRAVE MANHAMPTON ARE JUST BEATEN

Newchester 3 Manhampton 2

Manhampton were very unlucky to lose this match.

They were much the better team. Two great goals by Brown and Green put them 2–0 up at half time.

In the second half they scored two more goals. But the referee would not let them count. No one could see what was wrong with them.

The crowd could not believe it when the referee gave Newchester two penalty kicks. The Manhampton goalkeeper nearly saved them both.

In the final minute Newchester scored a shock winner. One of their players hit a hopeful shot. It was going well wide. But it hit the referee, bounced up into the face of Jones and went into his own goal.

It is the year AD 3000. Some students have been given a project to do called: 'Life in the 1990s'.

But they have a problem. There was an earthquake and nearly all the sources were lost. Only two sources were saved.

Source A

A photograph from the 1990s.

A photograph from the 1990s.

Questions

You are a student in AD 3000. You are trying to find out about 'Life in the 1990s'.

1 Look at Source A.
   What sort of clothes did people wear in the 1990s?

2 Look at Source B.
   What does it tell you about life in the 1990s?

3 What do Sources A and B not tell you about the 1990s?

Learning about history
Remember!

1 There are different kinds of **sources**. They give us clues (or evidence) about the past.

2 Written sources can be one-sided or biased.

3 Sometimes there are not enough sources to tell us the whole story.

What modern historians think

Historians think that Rome started near the river Tiber in Italy. There were seven villages, built on seven hills. Farmers lived in the villages. The villages grew together to become the city of Rome. This happened about 700 years before Jesus Christ was born.

Archaeologists have found pottery and round holes where the posts of the farmers' wooden huts used to be.

What the Romans said

The Romans told the story of Romulus and Remus to say how Rome started. You can read it on page 13. The story was passed down through the years.

Some of the story may be true, but other bits were made up to make it more exciting.

All Roman schoolchildren were told the story. The children loved to hear it. It made them think that Rome was a wonderful city. It made them proud to be Romans.

Rome was built on the river Tiber in Italy.

Source A

A statue of the she-wolf. She is feeding Romulus and Remus.

Questions

All the answers are on page 12.

1 In which country is Rome?

2 On which river was Rome built?

3 How do historians say Rome started?

4 What story did the Romans tell to say how Rome started?

5 Why were Roman schoolchildren told this story?

THE STORY OF ROMULUS AND REMUS

This is the story that was told to Roman children.

There was once a city called Alba Longa. It was on the banks of the river Tiber. It was ruled by King Numitor. He was driven from power by his wicked brother, Amulius.

Numitor's daughter was Rhea Silvia. She married Mars, the god of war. Rhea gave birth to twin boys. She called them Romulus and Remus.

Amulius was angry about this. He ordered the boys to be drowned. But the servant who was told to do this took pity on them. He left them floating in a cradle on the river.

The boys were found by a she-wolf. She let them feed on her milk. Then a shepherd found the boys. He took them home and brought them up.

When the boys grew up, they heard what Amulius had done to them. They were angry. They attacked Alba Longa. Amulius was killed.

Romulus and Remus said they would build a new city. They argued about where it should be built.

They agreed that whoever saw a vulture first in the sky could choose the place for the city. Remus said he saw a vulture first. But Romulus said he was the winner because he had seen twelve.

Romulus started to build the city on the Palatine hill. It had a wall around it. Remus was angry. He jumped over the wall to show that he did not think much of his brother's city. Romulus was so cross that he killed Remus.

The new city was finished in 753 BC. It was called Rome after Romulus.

Romulus was the first king of Rome. He died when he disappeared during a big storm. This happened in front of all the people of Rome.

Afterwards, Romulus became a god.

Rome ruled by kings

At first Rome was ruled by kings. The last king was called **Tarquinius Superbus** (Tarquin the Proud). The people did not like him. They drove him out of Rome in 509 BC.

Rome becomes a republic

The people said they did not want to be ruled by kings any more. Rome now became a **republic**. A republic is a place which does not have a king ruling.

Rome becomes powerful

Rome grew into the most powerful city in the world.

The Romans built a huge **empire**. An empire is when one country takes over and rules a lot of other countries.

The Roman Empire grew up slowly in four stages.

Stage 1: Rome takes over Italy

Rome started to take over other cities in Italy. By 265 BC Rome ruled most of Italy.

Roman land

ITALY
CORSICA
• Rome
SARDINIA
Mediterranean Sea
SICILY
Carthage •

N
S

| 0 | 300 miles |
| 0 | 400 km |

Rome ruled most of Italy by 265 BC.

HORATIUS THE HERO

The Romans loved to tell stories about brave people. One story was about a Roman soldier called Horatius Cocles (Horatio the One-Eyed).

Rome was being attacked by the Etruscans. They had to capture only one bridge to get into Rome. Horatius stopped the Etruscans from getting on to the bridge. He fought them off on his own. When he grew tired he jumped off the bridge and swam to the Roman side.

The Etruscans cheered but when they charged on to the bridge, it collapsed. They all fell into the river. The Romans had been chopping the bridge down while Horatius was fighting!

Horatius was a hero and was given a lot of land.

Stage 2: Rome beats Carthage

Carthage was a powerful city in north Africa. It ruled large parts of Africa and Spain. Carthage sold goods to the people who lived there.

Rome also started to sell goods to other countries. The Romans started to grow rich. Carthage did not like this. So the two cities went to war.

There were three wars between Rome and Carthage.

- **War 1 (264–241 BC).** The Romans won and took land from Carthage.
- **War 2 (218–201 BC).** Hannibal of Carthage took an army into Italy. The Romans beat him.
- **War 3 (149–146 BC).** The Romans burned the city of Carthage down. The Romans now ruled a big part of north Africa.

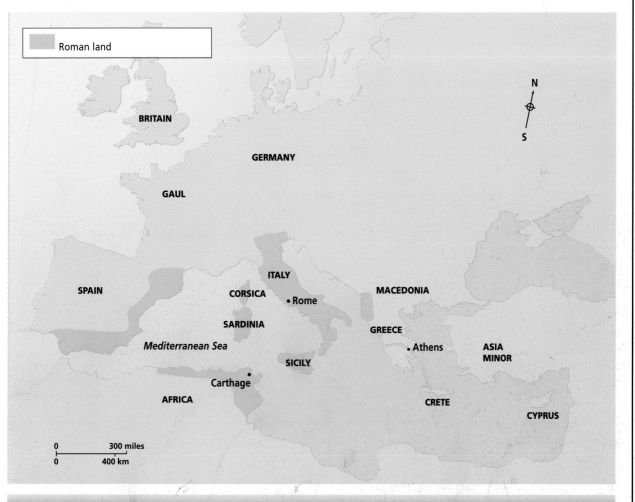

The start of the Roman Empire. This shows the land ruled by Rome after the second war against Carthage.

Stage 3: The Roman Empire grows

The Romans went on to capture more countries.

By **121 BC** the Romans had taken over Greece and Asia Minor (modern-day Turkey).

Stage 4: The Empire is completed

By **AD 120** the Romans had won more land in Asia, Africa and Britain. The Empire was now at its biggest.

Each country in the Empire was ruled by a Roman governor.

Each country was made to pay **taxes** to Rome.

Rome became very rich.

Source A

Written by a Roman historian.

The gods want Rome to be the most powerful city in the world.

No one will be able to beat the armies of Rome.

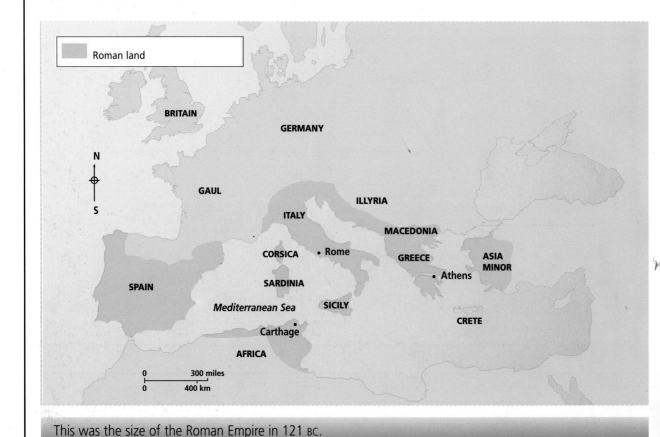

This was the size of the Roman Empire in 121 BC.

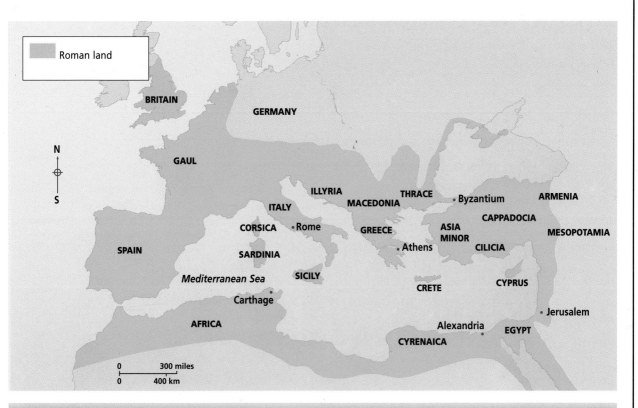

Key: Roman land

BRITAIN
GERMANY
GAUL
ILLYRIA
THRACE
Byzantium
ARMENIA
MACEDONIA
ITALY
CAPPADOCIA
CORSICA · Rome
GREECE
ASIA MINOR
MESOPOTAMIA
SPAIN
· Athens
CILICIA
SARDINIA
Mediterranean Sea
SICILY
CRETE
CYPRUS
Carthage
· Jerusalem
AFRICA
Alexandria
EGYPT
CYRENAICA

0 — 300 miles
0 — 400 km

The Roman Empire at its biggest in AD 120.

No more land to be taken

In AD 120 Emperor Hadrian said the Empire was big enough. If it got any bigger, it would be too hard to run. Hadrian said that no more land was to be taken.

He built Hadrian's Wall across the north of Britain. The wall was the northern border of the Roman Empire.

The Empire is divided

As time went on, the Romans found it harder to defend the Empire from attack.

In AD 285 the Empire was divided into two parts. This made it easier to run and defend.

Questions

Read **Rome becomes powerful** on page 14.

1 Write out these sentences, filling in the gaps. Use the words from the box.

Rome grew into a powerful _____. It took over many _____ and made them part of the Roman _____.

countries	Empire	city

2 Look at page 15.
Which city did Rome beat?

3 Read **No more land to be taken** on page 17.

   a Who said no more land was to be taken?
   b Why did he say this?
   c What did he build across northern Britain?

How do we know about Hannibal?

A Roman writer called **Livy** wrote about Hannibal's invasion of Italy. We still have Livy's books today.

Who was Hannibal?

Hannibal came from Carthage. You can find Carthage on the map on page 19. His father was called **Hamilcar**. In the first war between Carthage and Rome, Hamilcar was beaten in battle.

He was angry and wanted revenge. Hamilcar made Hannibal swear an oath that one day he would beat the Romans.

Hannibal joins the army

Hannibal joined the army in Carthage and became a good general.

He was strong and brave.

Hannibal became the leader of the army.

Hannibal decides to invade Italy

In 218 BC a second war started between Carthage and Rome.

Hannibal decided to invade Italy. But he could not go across the sea because the Romans had a better navy. The Romans would be able to sink Hannibal's ships. Hannibal would have to go the long way round.

The journey to Italy

Hannibal said he would march through Spain and France. Then he would cross some large mountains called the Alps and march into Italy.

This was a journey of 1,500 miles. He set off with 100,000 men and 37 war elephants.

Source A

A statue of Hannibal.

It was found in a town in Italy.

LIVY (59 BC–AD 17)

Livy was a rich Roman. He wrote a book about the history of Rome. It was used a lot in Roman schools.

Some people do not trust what he wrote. This is because he told only the Roman side of the story.

Danger at every turn

On the journey, Hannibal had to fight off attacks from fierce tribes.

When they came to a big river, the elephants were floated across on huge rafts.

The Alps are reached

After crossing the river Rhône in France, they came to the Alps. Hannibal's men were frightened.

But Hannibal told them not to be cowards.

Huge rafts were used to get the elephants across rivers.

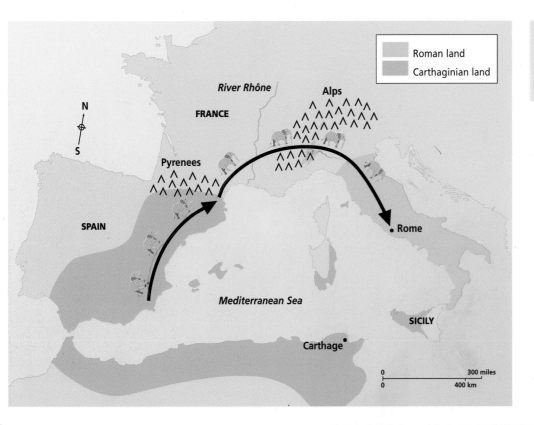

Hannibal's journey to Italy.

Roman land
Carthaginian land

River Rhône

Alps

FRANCE

N
S

Pyrenees

SPAIN

Rome

Mediterranean Sea

SICILY

Carthage

| 0 | 300 miles |
| 0 | 400 km |

Crossing the Alps

Hannibal's army struggled to the top of the mountains. It was hard going. Hannibal told his men it would be easier on the way down.

But it turned out to be even harder! The path down was very steep. Many men and animals slipped and died.

Then a huge boulder blocked their way. The boulder was bigger than a house. There seemed to be no way round it.

It looked as if their journey was at an end. But Hannibal had other ideas. His men started to break up the boulder (see box).

After the boulder had been broken up, the army was able to reach Italy.

It had taken them fifteen days to cross the Alps. Many men died on the way.

How the boulder was broken up

1 Vinegar was poured on to the boulder.

2 The acid in the vinegar helped to break up the boulder.

3 The men smashed the boulder with hammers.

4 After four days the boulder was smashed to pieces and the army was able to move on.

A modern painting of Hannibal's elephants crossing the Alps.

Source B

Panic in Rome

The people of Rome heard that Hannibal was on his way. They were very scared. But Hannibal did not have enough men or weapons to capture the city.

The Battle of Cannae

The Romans decided to fight Hannibal. But they were badly beaten in the Battle of Cannae.

Shocking scenes

There were terrible scenes after the battle. Thousands of Roman soldiers lay dying. They called out for people to cut their throats because they wanted to be put out of their misery.

At last Hannibal is beaten

By now Hannibal was running very short of supplies. So he had to go back to Carthage.

In 202 BC the Romans attacked Carthage. Hannibal was beaten in the fighting. Hannibal killed himself by taking poison.

The Romans celebrate

The Romans had been given a big scare by Hannibal. They were thankful he had not captured Rome.

For years afterwards, schoolchildren were told the story of Hannibal.

His name was used to frighten naughty children. Teachers would shout:

Hannibal is at the gates.

This soon made the children behave!

Questions

1 Read **The journey to Italy** on page 18.

   a Which mountains did Hannibal cross to get to Italy?

   b How many miles was his journey?

2 Look at page 19. How did they get the elephants across rivers?

3 Read **At last Hannibal is beaten**.

   a Why did Hannibal go back to Carthage?

   b How did he kill himself?

4 Read the box about **Livy** on page 18. Livy wrote about Hannibal's journey. Would you trust what he wrote?

3.1 THE ROMAN ARMY

Control of the Empire

People were frightened to fight the Romans. This was because the Romans had a very strong army. It hardly ever lost a battle. So the Romans kept control of the Empire.

Legions and centuries

- The biggest group in the Roman army was the **legion**.

- A legion had about 5,000 soldiers. They were called **legionaries**.

- A legion was commanded by a **legate**.

- A legion was divided into ten **cohorts**.

- A cohort was divided up into six **centuries**. Each century was under the command of a **centurion**.

Standards

Each century had its own badge or **standard**.

It was carried by the best soldier in the century.

It was a great honour to carry the standard.

Each legion also had a imperial standard, which was an eagle.

It was carried into battle by a standard-bearer. If the standard was captured in battle, it was a huge disgrace.

Source A

Written by a Roman in the 1st century AD.

A centurion called Luculius was killed by his own men. They hated him because he was so cruel.

The men called him 'give me another', because this is what he said each time he broke a stick hitting a soldier.

How to make a Roman legion

Step 1   Take eight men and form them into a group called a tent.

Step 2   Join ten tents together into a century of 80 men under the command of a centurion.

Step 3   Put six centuries together to make a cohort of 480 men.

CENTURY	CENTURY	CENTURY
1	2	3
CENTURY	CENTURY	CENTURY
4	5	6

Step 4   Put ten cohorts together to make 4,800 men. Add about 500 clerks and skilled tradesmen and you have a legion.

How the Roman army was organised.

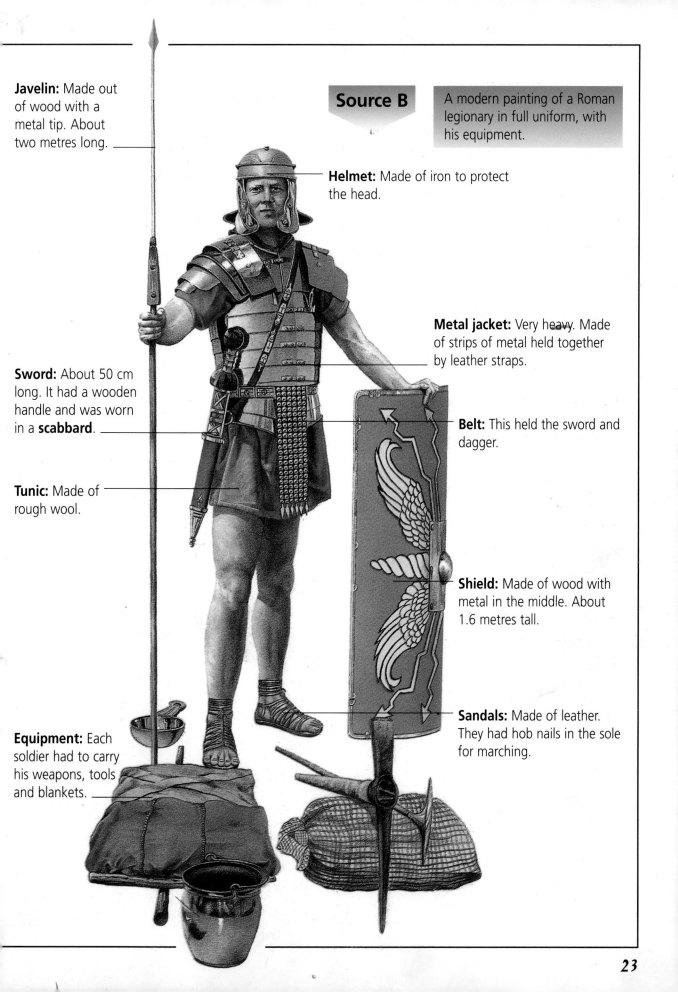

Javelin: Made out of wood with a metal tip. About two metres long.

Helmet: Made of iron to protect the head.

Metal jacket: Very heavy. Made of strips of metal held together by leather straps.

Sword: About 50 cm long. It had a wooden handle and was worn in a **scabbard**.

Belt: This held the sword and dagger.

Tunic: Made of rough wool.

Shield: Made of wood with metal in the middle. About 1.6 metres tall.

Sandals: Made of leather. They had hob nails in the sole for marching.

Equipment: Each soldier had to carry his weapons, tools and blankets.

Joining the Roman army

There were three sorts of soldiers in the Roman army:
Centurions
Legionaries and
Auxiliaries

Becoming a legionary

To become a legionary a person had to be:

A Roman citizen

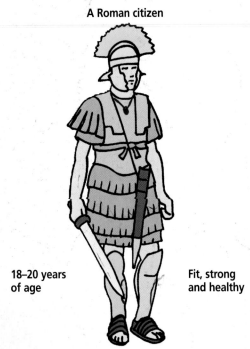

18–20 years of age

Fit, strong and healthy

Each legionary had to swear an oath of loyalty. They joined up for 25 years.

Training legionaries

The centurions trained the legionaries and were often very cruel to them. The training was very hard, so the legionaries had to be very fit and strong.

Three times a month the legionaries were sent on long marches. They were made to carry heavy packs. It was very tiring.

Legionaries were taught to:

- march in straight lines
- use a sword and shield
- throw the javelin.

Auxiliaries

Some soldiers in the army were called **auxiliaries**. They were soldiers who came from countries the Romans had conquered.

Special skills

The auxiliaries had special skills. They were very good at:

- fighting on horseback
- using a bow and arrow
- using a sling to shoot stones
- fighting with a sword.

Duties

Auxiliaries were used for patrolling and making quick raids on the enemy.

They were not as well trained as the legionaries. So they did not fight in big battles.

Length of service

Auxiliaries served for 25 years. When they left the army, they could become Roman citizens.

Source D

The tombstone of Marcus Favonius Facilis.

MARCUS FAVONIUS FACILIS

- Facilis was a centurion in the Twentieth Legion.

- His tombstone was found near Colchester.

- It had been broken into pieces, but it has been mended.

- It gives us a good idea of the uniform worn by a centurion.

- He has the centurion's stick in his right hand. The stick was used for beating soldiers.

Questions

1 Look at the picture on page 23.

   a Write down three weapons carried by a Roman legionary.

   b Write down three things which he had for protection.

   c Why did his sandals have hobnails in them?

2 Read **Training legionaries**.

   a Who trained the legionaries?

   b What was the training like?

3 Read Source A on page 22.
Why was Luculius killed by the soldiers?

4 Read **Standards** on page 22.
What was a standard?

Good discipline

The Romans were very orderly and disciplined. They *never* ran away from the battlefield.

Fighting a battle

1 The Roman army lined up like this:

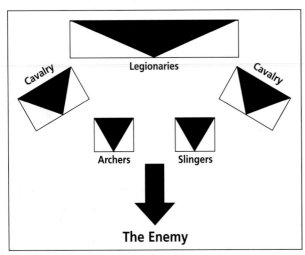

2 Before the battle started, stones and arrows were fired at the enemy.

3 Soldiers marched up close to the enemy and threw their javelins.

4 Soldiers then charged using their swords and shields.

Attacking forts

The Romans were very good at smashing down the walls of forts.

They had excellent weapons and ways for doing this.

1 Catapults

Small catapults fired arrows with a sharp metal point.

Large catapults fired stones. Some of these stones were huge. One soldier had his head knocked off by a big stone. His head landed over 500 metres away!

Source A

This person was killed by an arrow fired by a catapult. You can still see the arrowhead in his spine!

2 Battering rams

These were used to break down walls. They were made from huge tree trunks, with a large metal point at the end.

3 The tortoise formation

Often the Romans joined shields above their heads to form a shape like a tortoise. The shields protected the men from arrows and spears fired at their heads.

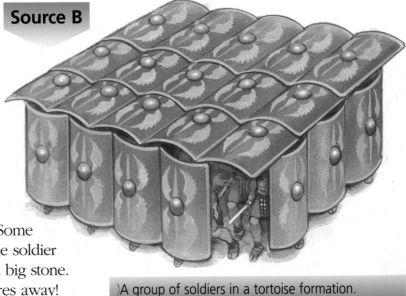

Source B

A group of soldiers in a tortoise formation.

4 Siege towers

These were made of wood. They were pushed up to the walls of the fort. From the top soldiers threw javelins at the enemy. They then climbed over the wall.

Roman soldiers attack a fort from inside a siege tower. Note the arrows being shot from the top, and the battering ram at the bottom of the tower.

Source C

The army had plenty of work to do in peacetime.

Army work

- Many hours were spent training and doing boring jobs (see Source A).
- When the army moved, the soldiers had to build a new camp.
- When a new country was conquered, the soldiers had to build forts.

Building work

- The army built many miles of road. The roads were straight and had cobblestones on top.

Source A

A list of jobs done by Roman soldiers in peacetime.

- **Digging ditches**
- **Cleaning the barracks**
- **Cleaning boots**
- **Mending weapons.**

How a Roman road was made

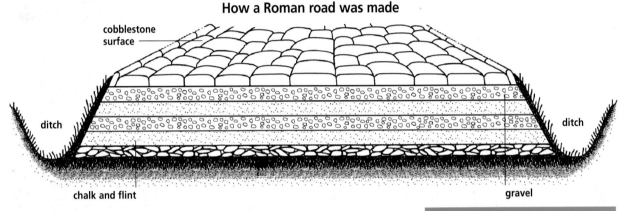

cobblestone surface

ditch

ditch

chalk and flint

gravel

- The army built Hadrian's Wall, which stretched across northern Britain.

A Roman carving showing soldiers building a fort.

Source B

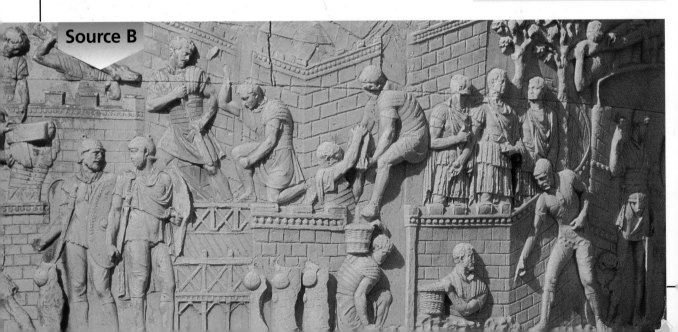

Fun and games

When they were not working, the soldiers had to make their own fun and amusements. They liked gambling games. They played dice and a form of noughts and crosses. Board games were also very popular (Source D).

Source C

From a letter to a Roman soldier. It was found at the fort of Vindolanda in Northumberland.

I have sent you some socks, two pairs of sandals and two pairs of underpants. I wish you the best of luck.

Source D

From *The Times* newspaper, 25 September 1996.

ROMAN BOARD GAME FOUND

A board game played by the Romans has been found in a grave in Essex. The grave is 2,000 years old.

The game was found next to the bones of its owner. It had been buried with the owner so that he could have some fun in the afterlife. The pieces are laid out ready to play.

The excited archaeologist said:

'We found a whole row of blue pieces. Then we found the white pieces. It was like magic. Bits of the playing board are there too. The wooden bits of the board have rotted away, but the metal edges are still there.'

Glass beads

Hinge

55 cm

Wooden board

40 cm

Questions

1 Look at pages 26–7. Write down four things the Romans used to attack forts.

2 Read **Building work** on page 28. What two kinds of building work did the army do?

3 Look at page 29. How do we know that the Romans played board games?

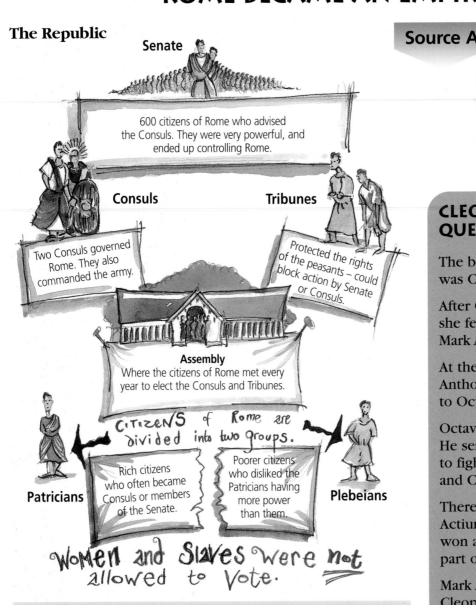

The Republic

Senate

600 citizens of Rome who advised the Consuls. They were very powerful, and ended up controlling Rome.

Consuls

Two Consuls governed Rome. They also commanded the army.

Tribunes

Protected the rights of the peasants – could block action by Senate or Consuls.

Assembly

Where the citizens of Rome met every year to elect the Consuls and Tribunes.

CITIZENS of Rome are divided into two groups.

Patricians

Rich citizens who often became Consuls or members of the Senate.

Plebeians

Poorer citizens who disliked the Patricians having more power than them.

WOMEN and SLAVES were not allowed to vote.

Rome was ruled by kings until 509 BC. After that Rome was a republic. A republic does not have a king. This is how the republic worked.

The Republic breaks down

By 100 BC the army had become very powerful. The Senate could not control the army. Some generals in the army wanted to get power.

They began fighting each other to see who could rule Rome. The most famous general who wanted to rule Rome was **Julius Caesar**.

Source A

CLEOPATRA – QUEEN OF EGYPT

The beautiful Cleopatra was Caesar's lover.

After Caesar's death, she fell in love with Mark Anthony in 41 BC.

At the time Mark Anthony was married to Octavian's sister.

Octavian was angry. He sent an army to Egypt to fight Mark Anthony and Cleopatra.

There was a sea battle at Actium in 31 BC. Octavian won and he made Egypt part of the Roman Empire.

Mark Anthony and Cleopatra then killed themselves.

Cleopatra was said to have put a snake on her chest. The snake gave her a poisonous bite.

Who was Julius Caesar?

Caesar was born in 100 BC. He came from a rich family. He was clever and good at sport. He was made a **Consul** in 59 BC, and then was put in charge of the Roman army in Gaul.

A coin with Caesar's head on it. The words mean 'Caesar dictator for life'.

Dictator for life

Caesar was a brilliant general. He beat the Gauls in battle many times and won more land for Rome. This made him very popular. He went back to Rome and was loudly cheered by the people.

Caesar was made dictator (ruler) for life. He was now the most powerful man in Rome.

Murder!

Some people in the Senate did not like Caesar. They thought he had too much power. They decided to murder him. On 15 March 44 BC, Caesar was stabbed to death in the Senate House. A Roman writer told how horrible it was:

A group of men crowded round Caesar. One held his shoulders and another stabbed him in the throat. He was stabbed 23 more times. Caesar was left lying dead. Then three of his slaves carried him home.

A contest for power

After this there was a contest between **Mark Anthony**, **Octavian** and **Lepidus** to see who should rule the Empire. Octavian won.

The first emperor

In 27 BC Octavian became the first emperor. The republic had ended. Octavian now called himself **Augustus**, which means 'respected one'. The cartoon on pages 32–33 tells you more about these events.

How much power did the emperors have?

From 27 BC Rome was ruled by an emperor.

The emperor was very powerful:

1 The emperor was in charge of the army.

2 The emperor picked the people to run the city of Rome.

3 The emperor picked the people to run the Empire.

4 The emperor was in charge of the money. He often spent it on such things as:

- gladiator fights
- free bread for the people
- higher wages for the army.

This made him popular and kept him in power.

509 BC

oh dear! There goes my income

TARQUINIUS IS TOO PROUD

OUT WITH TARQUINIUS

107. BC

509 BC Tarquinius Superbus, the last King of Rome, was driven out. Rome became a republic.

In 107 BC the Consul Marius opened up the army to all citizens. The army became too big for the Consuls and Senate to control.

27 BC Octavian was made Rome's first emperor, taking the name Augustus Caesar.

Mark Anthony fell in love with Cleopatra, the Queen of Egypt. He was married to Octavian's sister at the time. This made Octavian very angry.

EMPEROR OF ROME

MARK ANTHONY   LEPIDIUS

36 BC

31 BC

BATTLE REPORT
OCTAVIAN 1
LEPIDIUS 0

WEDDING SHOCK
MARK ANTHONY LEAVES NEW WIFE FOR OLD LOVE CLEOPATRA

Anybody seen my husband?

41 BC

DEAR CLEOPATRA
LOVE YOU SO MUCH
your boyfriend
Mark Anthony

In 31 BC Octavian defeated Mark Anthony in battle. Mark Anthony and Cleopatra committed suicide.

Julius Caesar was made Consul in 59 BC and put in charge of the Roman army in Gaul. He returned in 49 BC having beaten all the tribes of Gaul. Caesar started acting like a king. In 44 BC a group of Senators tried to save the republic by murdering Caesar.

Mark Anthony, Octavian and Lepidius divided the Empire between them. They became rivals.

Questions

1 Look at the cartoon.
  Copy these sentences. Fill in the gaps.

  a The last _____ was driven out in 509 BC.
  b Rome then became a _____.

2 Who became the first Roman emperor in 27 BC?

Disaster strikes Pompeii

Pompeii was a town in southern Italy. It was built near a volcano called Mount Vesuvius. The volcano had been quiet for hundreds of years.

Suddenly, on 24 August AD 79, the volcano blew up. The top of the volcano was blown hundreds of metres into the air. Ash and hot rocks fell on to the terrified people of Pompeii.

Poisonous gas

Many people were choked by poisonous gases and fumes from the volcano.

They could not breathe. They dropped to the ground and died.

Soon their bodies were covered under six metres of hot ashes.

Source A

The ruins of Pompeii. This was painted by an English artist in 1820.

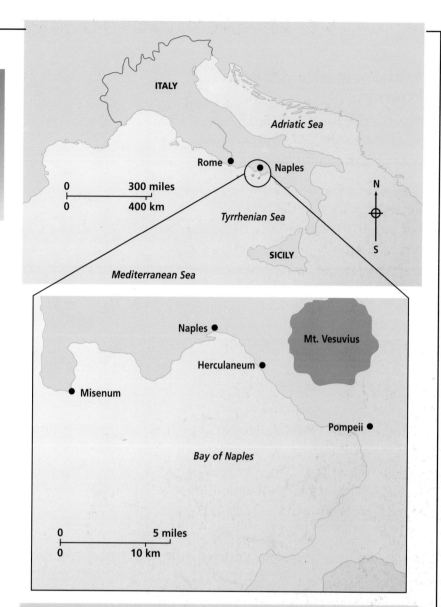

Pompeii and the Bay of Naples. Mount Vesuvius was very close.

Panic

There was panic as people tried to escape.

Some people tried to escape in boats. But the sea was very rough. Skeletons have been found near the water's edge.

Historians think the boats capsized and people were drowned.

Not many horse skeletons have been found at Pompeii. So it seems possible that some people rode to safety on horseback.

A terrible death

Pompeii was buried under a huge pile of ash and rocks. Thousands of men, women and children died a terrible death.

Archaeologists dig up Pompeii

Pompeii lay buried for 1,700 years. All that could be seen was a large mound of earth.

Archaeologists wanted to know what lay under the earth. So they began digging.

What buildings have been found?

By carefully digging up the ground, archaeologists have found:

- the town wall
- streets laid out in a grid
- the **forum** (market place)
- bath-houses
- two theatres
- a sports field with a swimming pool
- an **amphitheatre** (stadium).

The things found at Pompeii tell us a lot about how the Romans lived.

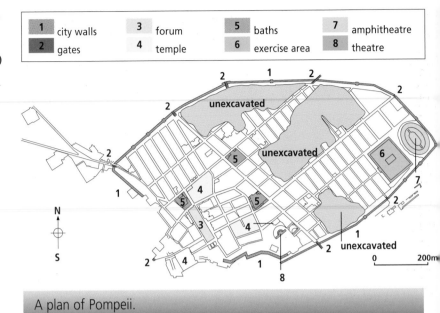

| 1 | city walls | 3 | forum | 5 | baths | 7 | amphitheatre |
| 2 | gates | 4 | temple | 6 | exercise area | 8 | theatre |

A plan of Pompeii.

Plaster-cast models of the dead

Archaeologists found signs of many dead bodies – people and animals. But their flesh had rotted away and left holes in the ash. Each hole was the same shape as a dead body.

The archaeologists poured liquid plaster into the holes. When the plaster went hard, it made a plaster-cast model of the dead body (see Sources C and D). A lot of these plaster-cast models have been made.

How big was Pompeii?

Archaeologists think that about 20,000 people lived in Pompeii.

The town covered an area of 64 hectares. The plan (above) shows you how the streets were laid out.

Source C

The body of a person who died in a street.

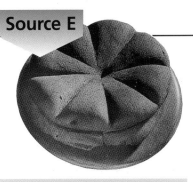

A loaf of bread from Pompeii. It looks perfect, but is rock hard!

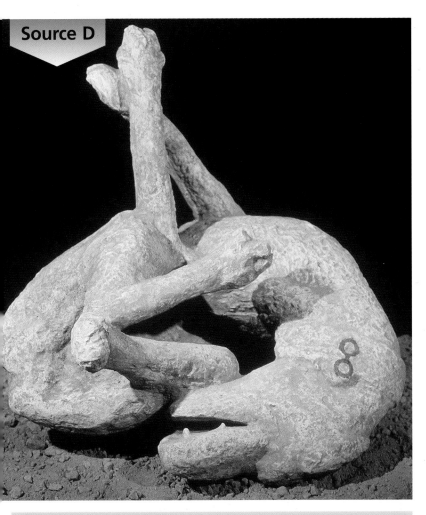

The body of a dog found at Pompeii. It had been chained up. It died trying to get free.

Last moments

Here are some of the dead people found at Pompeii. Archaeologists can tell what they were doing at the very moment they died.

- A beggar with a new pair of shoes found on a street corner
- Eighteen people huddled together in a cellar
- A woman with some fine jewels
- Two prisoners chained up in a cell
- Seven children killed when a baker's house fell on them.

Questions

1 Read **Disaster strikes Pompeii** on page 34.

   a Which volcano was near to Pompeii?
   b Write a sentence to say what happened in AD 79.
   c What fell on to the people?

2 Read **Poisonous gas** on page 34.

   How did the gas kill people?

3 Read Source B on page 35.

   Would you trust what this person tells us?

4 Look at pages 36 and 37.

   a Make a list of things that the archaeologists found at Pompeii.
   b Why are these things important to us today?

37

The wonderful city of Rome

Rome was a wonderful place. It was the largest city in the Empire. It had many large buildings, as well as temples, shops and public baths. Thousands of people visited Rome each year.

> **LARGE BUILDINGS IN ROME**
>
> **The Emperor's Palace** – where the emperor lived.
>
> **The Colosseum** – a large arena where the gladiators fought.
>
> **The Circus Maximus** – a track where chariot racing took place.

Houses of the rich

The rich people had big houses. They had central heating, painted walls, toilets, baths and large gardens. Many rich people also had a big villa in the countryside. They went there to get away from the heat and smell of the city.

Houses of the poor

Most of the people in Rome were poor. They lived in flats which were built close together. The flats were badly built. Each flat had only one or two rooms. They did not have an inside toilet or running water.

Source A

Poor people lived in flats like these.

A model of what historians think Rome looked like.

Source B

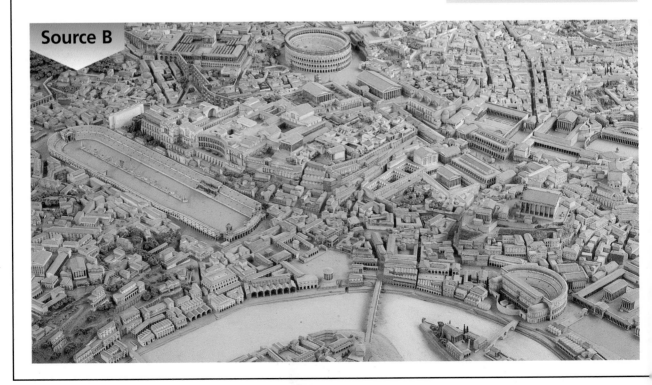

A visit to the public baths

There were public baths in every Roman town. They were cheap to enter. Even poor people could afford to go.

People loved going to the baths. As well as bathing, people played board games and chatted to their friends. The baths could be *very* noisy (see Source C).

A visit to the public toilets

Most people did not have a toilet in their home. So they had to use a public toilet.

People sat next to each other. There was no wall to separate them or a door to lock! They chatted to the next person as they went to the toilet (see Source D).

The Romans did not have toilet paper. Instead they used a sponge on the end of a stick. When they had finished with it, they washed it and handed it on to the next person!

Source C

This Roman lived above a public bath-house. He did not like the noise.

The baths are very noisy. It drives me mad.

People lifting weights grunt and groan.

When people have a massage you can hear the slap of the hands on bodies.

Some sing at the top of their voice in the bath.

Then there are the oafs who dive in the pool with the biggest splash they can make.

Source D

A public toilet being used by soldiers. This was drawn by a modern artist.

Questions

1 Why did a lot of people visit Rome?

2 Look at Source D. Was a visit to a public toilet in Roman times **a** the same as or **b** different from today?

Chariot racing

The Romans loved to have a day out at the chariot racing.

In Rome there was a big race track called the Circus Maximus.

It could hold about 250,000 people.

The races

There could be as many as twelve chariots in a race.

Each chariot was pulled by four horses. They did seven laps of the track, a distance of eight kilometres.

The racing was dangerous. There were many crashes. The drivers were often injured and some were even killed.

The crowd

The drivers wore different team colours. People had banners to show which driver they supported. They gambled lots of money on who would win the races.

The drivers

The best drivers were paid a lot of money.

Many drivers were slaves. If they earned a lot of money, they would buy their freedom.

The Games

In Rome there was another large stadium called the Colosseum. It was here that the Games were held.

Source A

A scene from a modern film called *Ben Hur*. It shows a chariot race.

Source B

This Roman did not like chariot races.

I am not interested in the races. Once you have seen one race, you have seen them all.

People only go to see the drivers' colours. They do not go to see the skill of the drivers or the speed of the horses.

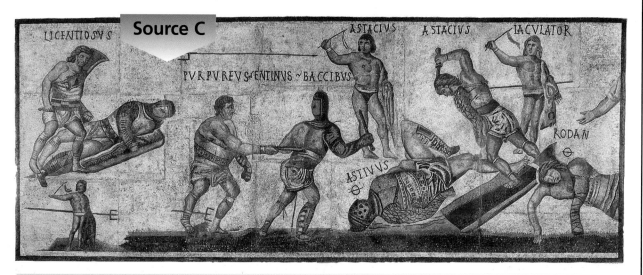

Source C

A Roman mosaic showing gladiators fighting.

The Games were made up of different things such as:

1 Animals doing tricks.

2 Hungry animals fighting to the death.

3 Animals being hunted in the arena and then killed.

4 Criminals fighting lions and tigers. The criminals did not have any weapons and were usually killed.

Gladiator fights

Gladiators were slaves, prisoners of war or criminals. They were trained to fight to the death.

If a gladiator was wounded, he raised his finger. This showed that he was asking for mercy.

If he had fought well, he was allowed to live. If he had fought badly, he was killed by the other gladiator. Most fights ended in death.

Source D

This Roman did not like the Games.

All I saw was murder. The fights are cruel and always end in death.

The crowd is very bloodthirsty. People shout out: 'Kill him! Beat him! Burn him! What a coward he is!'

Questions

1 Read **Chariot racing** and **The Games**. Copy these sentences. Fill in the gaps.

   a Chariot racing was held at the _____ _____.
   b The Games were held at the _____.

2 Read **Gladiator fights**.

   a What did a gladiator do to show he wanted mercy?
   b What happened if he had fought well?
   c What happened if he had fought badly?

3 Read Source D.
   'All Romans were cruel and bloodthirsty.' Is this statement true or false?

What was a villa?

A villa was a big house in the countryside. Only rich Romans lived in villas. Many villas were on a farm.

Inside a villa

Most villas had lots of rooms. There were beautiful paintings on the walls. There were **mosaics** on the floor. Mosaics were made up of lots of tiny pieces of coloured stone. They were made into a pattern.

Many villas had a **hypocaust**. This was a type of central heating.

Meals

The villa owner was rich. He and his family lived a good life. They ate three meals a day:

1 **Breakfast**: A light snack of bread and honey.

2 **Mid-morning snack**: Bread and cheese.

3 **Dinner**: This was the main meal of the day. It was eaten in the late afternoon.

People laid on couches to eat the food. They did not use knives and forks. Instead, they ate with their fingers!

If the owner had guests, the meal would be eight courses. Dishes such as pheasant, partridge and stuffed dormouse were served.

If they were full, people left the room and made themselves sick. Then they carried on eating!

Ordinary people in the countryside

We do not know much about ordinary Romans. Not much was written about them. Most of their houses have rotted away.

Houses

Most ordinary people in the countryside lived in small, round houses with a thatched roof. The roof had a hole in it for the smoke to get out. The floor was made of beaten earth.

Meals

Ordinary country people ate porridge made from wheat. Spices and vegetables were put into the porridge. This gave it more flavour.

These people did not eat fish or meat very often. Meat was very dear.

Questions

1 Read **What was a villa?**
Copy these sentences. Fill in the gaps.

A villa was _____.
Only _____ _____ lived in villas.

2 Read **Inside a villa**.

a What would be seen on the walls?
b What would be seen on the floor?
c What was a hypocaust?

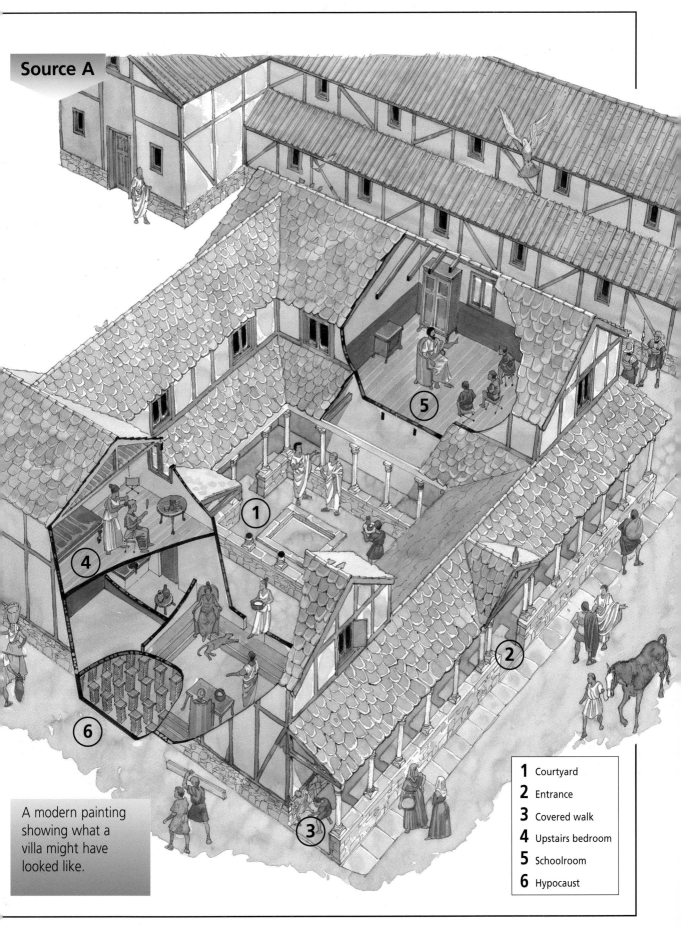

Source A

A modern painting showing what a villa might have looked like.

1	Courtyard
2	Entrance
3	Covered walk
4	Upstairs bedroom
5	Schoolroom
6	Hypocaust

Danie wn James4 Effa.

Roman villas had their own baths. Baths had a lot of rooms. Each room had a different purpose. The Romans really enjoyed having a bath.

4 They went into the hot steam room. The bathers rubbed perfumed oil on their skin. As they sweated, they took off the oil with a scraper called a **strigil**.

Source A

5 Finally they plunged into a cold bath.

1 The bathers took off their clothes. They put sandals on so they would not burn their feet.

2 The bathers did some exercises.

A modern painting of a Roman bath-house. You can see the hypocaust furnace outside the main building.

3 They went into the warm room.

Keeping tidy – men

Rich men were clean shaven. Their faces were shaved by a slave or they went to a barber. Poor men could not afford to go to a barber. So they usually had a beard.

Many men were scared of going bald. They rubbed in potions which they thought would stop their hair falling out. One potion was made of rat droppings!

Keeping tidy – women

Women often changed the style of their hair. Some wore wigs to look good. They wore face creams made from milk and flour. They also wore scent which came from India.

Question

Are these statements **true** or **false**?

- The Romans were dirty people.
- The Romans did not care what they looked like.

Explain your answers.

Source C

An oil can and strigil.

Source D

A Roman complains about his barber.

If you want to stay alive, keep away from Antiochus the barber.

I did not get the scars on my chin from boxing. Nor was I scratched by the sharp nails of an angry wife.

The scars came from the razor of Antiochus.

Source B

The ruins of a hypocaust at Chedworth Roman villa.

Source E

From a Roman poem.

Galla, you get your beauty from the chemist. Your hair is dyed with German herbs. You have false teeth which you keep in a box – just like your dresses.

A Roman family

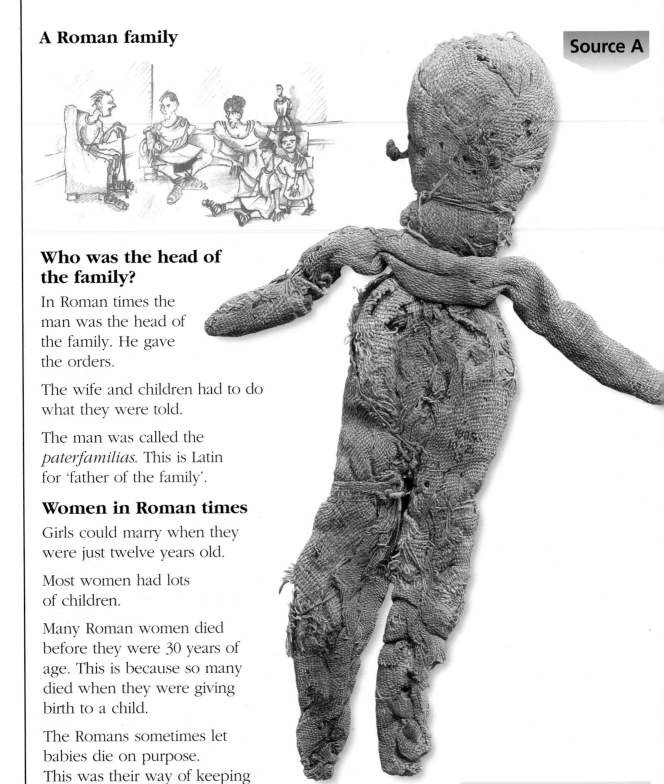

Source A

Who was the head of the family?

In Roman times the man was the head of the family. He gave the orders.

The wife and children had to do what they were told.

The man was called the *paterfamilias*. This is Latin for 'father of the family'.

Women in Roman times

Girls could marry when they were just twelve years old.

Most women had lots of children.

Many Roman women died before they were 30 years of age. This is because so many died when they were giving birth to a child.

The Romans sometimes let babies die on purpose. This was their way of keeping the population down (see Source B).

Roman children played with similar toys to us. This rag doll, from Roman times, was found in Egypt.

Poor children

Children from poor homes had a hard life. They were sent out to work at an early age. Some poor children were sold as slaves to rich families.

Rich children

Children from rich homes had a good life. They had lots of toys to play with. Archaeologists have found dolls' houses, rocking horses and rag dolls.

Girls were taught to be housewives. Boys spent time running and throwing spears. This would later help them to get into the Roman army.

Schools

Rich children started school when they were seven. The teachers were strict. They often used the cane.

Lessons lasted from dawn until noon. The same teacher taught all subjects.

Just like today the children were taught reading, writing and arithmetic.

Poor children did not go to school. They grew up unable to read and write.

Source B

MASS BABIES' GRAVE FOUND IN ISRAEL

Scientists have found a mass grave of over 100 babies in Israel. They think the grave was dug in the 4th century AD. Israel was then part of the Roman Empire.

The babies were only one or two days old.

A scientist said: 'It was normal in Roman time to let babies die. They did it to keep the population down.'

From the *Guardian* newspaper, 16 January 1997.

Questions

1 Read Source B.

   a Where was the grave found?
   b How many dead babies were in it?
   c How old were the babies when they died?
   d Why had the babies been allowed to die by the Romans?

2 Read **Poor children** and **Rich children**.

   a What was life like for poor children?
   b What was life like for rich children?

3 Read **Schools**.
   Make a list of how Roman schools were different from schools today.

6.6 SLAVES AND GODS

Large numbers of slaves

There were over 400,000 slaves in Rome. Only rich people had slaves. The poor could not afford slaves.

Slave markets

When the Romans captured a country, they took many prisoners. The prisoners were taken to Rome. Here they were sold to be slaves.

People would bid money to buy the slaves. It was rather like buying furniture or an animal!

What work did slaves do?

Source A

A Roman mosaic of a boy slave.

Strong men worked on farms or built roads

Clever people worked as doctors or teachers

Others worked as maids, gardeners and cooks

Life as a slave

Some slaves were treated badly. Others had a better life than if they had been free.

Slaves who ran away were punished. If a slave murdered his owner, all the other slaves in the house were put to death.

Slaves who worked hard were often given their freedom. They could then buy land, but they were not allowed to vote.

Source B

A nobleman praises another Roman for being kind to his slaves.

I have heard you are kind to your slaves. I am pleased about this. They may be slaves, but they are also humans as well.

A statue of the Roman god Mars.

Some Roman gods

Jupiter:	The king of the gods
Juno:	The queen of the gods
Mars:	The god of war
Mercury:	The messenger of the gods
Neptune:	The god of the sea
Venus:	The goddess of love

Many gods

The Romans had lots of different gods. They built temples to their gods.

Gifts and sacrifices

There were festivals on special days for each god.

People wanted to please the gods. So they gave gifts of flowers and fruit to the gods. They sometimes killed an animal as a **sacrifice**.

Cruel treatment of Christians

Some people in the Roman Empire became Christians.

Christians did not believe in the Roman gods. They believed in Jesus Christ.

The emperor said it was against the law to be a Christian.

Christians were forced to pray in secret. If the Romans found out, the Christians were cruelly treated.

Many Christians were killed when they were made to fight wild animals in the Colosseum. Most Romans thought this was good fun!

Christianity allowed in Rome

In AD 324 **Emperor Constantine** became a Christian. Many Romans copied him.

In AD 380 Christianity became the main religion of the Empire. Other religions were not allowed after this.

Questions

1 What kinds of job did slaves do?

2 Copy this sentence. Fill in the gaps. Use the words in the box.

   At first the Romans had _____ _____, but they later became _____.

Christians	Many gods

7.1 ROMAN BRITAIN

Julius Caesar

Julius Caesar was in charge of the Roman army in Gaul (modern-day France).

Why did Caesar invade Britain?

He was angry that the British had helped the Gauls to fight the Romans.

He wanted the gold, silver and tin in Britain.

He would be liked in Rome if he beat the British.

Caesar lands in Kent, 55 BC

Caesar's small army arrived in Kent in 55 BC.

The British were waiting for them on the beach. They had spears and looked very fierce. At first the Romans were too frightened to get out of their boats (see Source B).

When they finally landed, the Romans marched a few miles inland. They took some prisoners.

Then a storm damaged their ships. The Romans mended the ships and sailed back to Gaul.

Caesar returns to Britain, 54 BC

Caesar went back to Britain in 54 BC. This time he had a bigger army. He marched further inland and beat the British in a battle. Caesar captured some prisoners and took money from the British.

But Caesar was worried that there would a rebellion in Gaul while he was away. So he decided to go back to Gaul.

It was to be almost 100 years before the Romans invaded Britain again.

Source A

A modern painting of Julius Caesar's invasion of Britain in 55 BC.

Source B

Caesar tells what happened when he came to Britain in 55 BC.

My soldiers were not used to landing from boats and paddling on to a beach.

They did not want to get out of the boats.

The British threw spears and galloped into the sea.

Then our standard-bearer shouted: 'Do you want us to lose our eagle?'

He jumped out of the boat and walked towards the British. The other soldiers followed him.

Questions

1 Read **Why did Caesar invade Britain?**
   Write down one reason why Caesar went to Britain.

2 Copy these sentences. Fill in the gaps. Use the words in the box.

   Caesar first went to Britain in _____.
   He went back _____ year later in _____.

54 BC	one	55 BC

3 Read Source B.
   Why do you think the Romans were frightened to land?

Why did the Romans invade Britain in AD 43?

In AD 43 the **Emperor Claudius** ordered the Roman army to invade Britain again. Why did he do this?

1 He wanted Britain to be part of the Roman Empire.
2 He wanted to show people he was strong.
3 He was angry with the British for helping the Gauls.

Demons!

The Roman soldiers did not want to invade Britain. They thought they would sail off the edge of the world. Stories went round that Britain was a land full of demons. The soldiers had to be talked into getting off the ships.

The Romans arrive in Britain

A Roman army of 40,000 men finally landed in Kent.

The British put up a good fight. Their leader was **Caractacus**. He was beaten by the Romans in a battle near the river Medway. Caractacus fled to Wales.

The Romans then captured Colchester. Claudius was very pleased. His two-year-old son was renamed Britannicus.

Source A

A speech made in Rome by Caractacus. After the speech he was allowed to live.

If I had not put up such a good fight, your victory would not look so great.

If you kill me, you will look very cruel.

If you let me live, people will say that the Romans are kind and can show mercy.

THE HEAD OF CLAUDIUS

In 1907, a boy swimming in a river in Suffolk spotted something on the river bed.

He dived down to see what it was, and pulled out this bronze head of Claudius!

It is now in the British Museum, London.

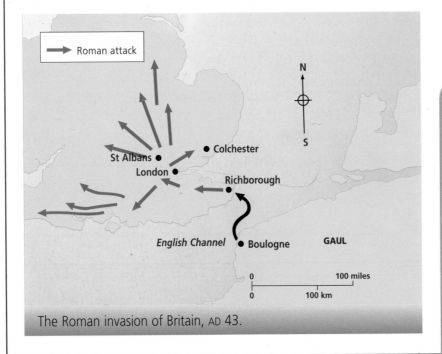

The Roman invasion of Britain, AD 43.

Maiden Castle in Dorset. This was a British fort. It was captured by the Romans.

Caractacus is captured

The Romans captured Caractacus. He was tied up and taken to Rome. He was paraded in the streets and made fun of. Claudius said he was going to kill Caractacus. But Caractacus made such a brave speech that he was allowed to live (see Source A).

The Romans conquer more of Britain

The Romans soon had the east and south of Britain under control.

But it took longer to conquer the west and north of Britain. The land there is hilly, which makes it hard for fighting.

Emperor Hadrian decided to build a wall to protect the land that the Romans had captured. Hadrian's Wall was the northern border of the Roman Empire.

Questions

1 Look at page 52.

   a Who ordered the invasion of Britain in AD 43?
   b Who was the British leader?
   c Which town did the Romans capture?

2 Read **The Romans conquer more of Britain**.

   a Which part of Britain was conquered quickly?
   b Why was it harder for the Romans to conquer the west and north of Britain?

Queen **Boudica** was one of the British leaders.

The Romans did not like her. They wanted her land and money.

Boudica was flogged by the Romans. They also stole from her palace.

Boudica wanted revenge.

Source A

Boudica was flogged by the Romans.

Boudica's revolt

Boudica attacked Colchester, where the Romans lived. Then she burned down St Albans and London. About 70,000 Romans were killed.

Boudica is beaten

The Romans were worried. They decided to fight a battle against Boudica.

Boudica had a much bigger army than the Romans. But the Romans fought well and Boudica was beaten.

After the battle, Boudica poisoned herself. She did not want to be captured by the Romans.

Source B

Modern artists have tried to show what they thought Boudica looked like.

Source C

A Roman describes Boudica.

Boudica was a huge woman. She had long ginger hair down to her knees. She was frightening to look at.

She wore a coloured tunic with a thick cloak. She also wore a heavy gold necklace.

She shook a spear to frighten people.

Boudica: what's in a name?

The name of Boudica has been spelt differently throughout time.

1 The Romans spelt it as 'Boudicca'. They were wrong!

2 Medieval people spelt it as 'Boadicea'. This, too, was wrong!

3 We now know that 'Boudica' is the right spelling!

Source D

A statue of Boudica near the river Thames in London. Look at the spikes sticking out from the wheels of her chariot.

Source E

Boudica made a speech before going into battle.

I am fighting for my lost freedom and my bruised body.

The gods will give us revenge on the Romans.

We will fight fiercely and make a lot of noise. The Romans will not be able to stand up to us.

Source F

A Roman says how many died.

About 80,000 Britons were killed in the battle. Only 400 Romans were killed.

Questions

1 Read the top of page 54.
   Why did Boudica attack the Romans?

2 Read **Boudica is beaten** on page 54.

   a What did the Romans do?
   b What happened to Boudica?

3 Read Source C.
   What does it say about Boudica?

4 Look at Source B on page 54.
   Do you think the artist of Source B had read Source C?

Source A

Hadrian's Wall today.

Why was Hadrian's Wall built?

In AD 117, tribes from Scotland and the north of England attacked the Romans. They caused a lot of damage.

The Emperor Hadrian was worried. So he visited Britain. He saw that it would be very hard to conquer the Scots.

Hadrian decided to build a wall to keep the Scots out. The wall was built between Wallsend-on-Tyne and Bowness-on-Solway. It was 117 kilometres long.

Building the wall

It took thousands of soldiers five years to build the wall.

Success

The wall did its job well. It stopped the Scots from attacking. The wall was so well built that parts of it are still standing today (see Source A).

The five parts of the wall

1 The wall was 6 metres tall and 3 metres wide. It was built out of stone.

2 On the north side of the wall a huge ditch was dug. Attackers would have to cross this ditch before they got to the wall.

3 There was another ditch, or **vallum**, on the south side of the wall. This was not so deep. The Romans did not expect to be attacked from the south.

4 There was a fort every eight kilometres along the wall. Each fort had 500 soldiers. The forts also had workshops, food stores, barracks and a hospital.

5 Between the forts were **milecastles**. They held 100 men. Between the milecastles were **turrets**. These had two or three soldiers on watch. They would signal the forts if an attack was about to happen.

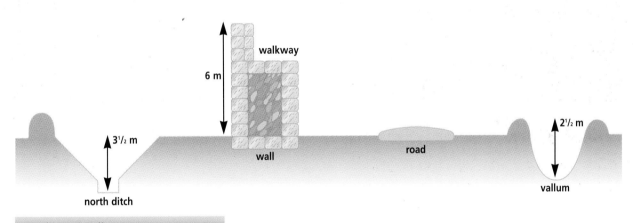

Hadrian's Wall.

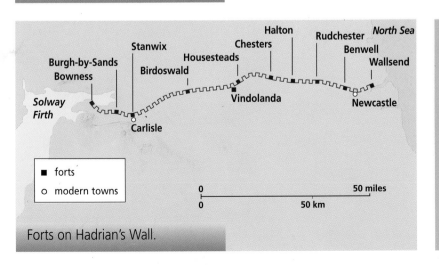

Forts on Hadrian's Wall.

Questions

1 Read **Why was Hadrian's Wall built?**

  a Write down a reason why the wall was built.

  b How long was the wall?

2 What can we learn from Source A about Hadrian's Wall?

7.5 VINDOLANDA – 'A TREASURE TROVE OF ROMAN HISTORY'

About Vindolanda

Vindolanda was a Roman fort near Hadrian's Wall.

In the 1970s, archaeologists dug up the fort. They found many interesting things which tell us a lot about the Romans.

The Vindolanda tablets

The archaeologists were very excited to find bits of wood called **tablets**. The tablets have writing on them.

Some of the tablets have rotted, but it is still possible to work out what they say.

The tablets tell us about life in the Roman army. Some are letters home from soldiers living in the fort.

The tablets are important because we have little else to tell us about ordinary Roman people.

Source A

A model of what a Roman kitchen may have looked like.

Source B

A list of food and drink from the Vindolanda tablets.

Wine, garlic, fish, pork, cereal, butter, deer, beer, spices, beans, goat, barley, lentils, honey, olives, oysters, eggs, bread, ham, plums, chicken, radishes, salt, pepper, semolina.

Source C

The ruined buildings at Vindolanda.

Source D

A pendant found at Vindolanda.

Source E

A child's sandal found at Vindolanda.

Source F

Writing from the Vindolanda tablets.

1 FROM CLAUDIA SEVERA TO SULPICIA LEPIDINA

I send greetings to Lepidina. It is my birthday. Make sure you come to see me, so the day will be more enjoyable.

2 A CALL FOR MERCY

I beg your majesty not to let me be beaten with a stick. I am innocent. I have done nothing wrong.

3 FROM SOLEMIS TO HIS BROTHER, PARIS

I send you greetings. I am very well. I hope you are well, too. You are very bad at writing. You have not sent me one single letter. I am a kinder person, so I am writing this letter to you.

Questions

1 Read **About Vindolanda** on page 58.

   a What was Vindolanda?
   b Where was Vindolanda?

2 Read **The Vindolanda tablets** on page 58.

   a What were the tablets made of?
   b What did they have on them?
   c What do the tablets tell us about?
   d Why are they important to us?

3 Look at Sources C, D and E. What does each source tell us about the Romans?

The end of the Roman Empire

The Roman Empire collapsed when it was attacked by fierce **barbarian** tribes.

By AD 476 the Roman Empire was at an end.

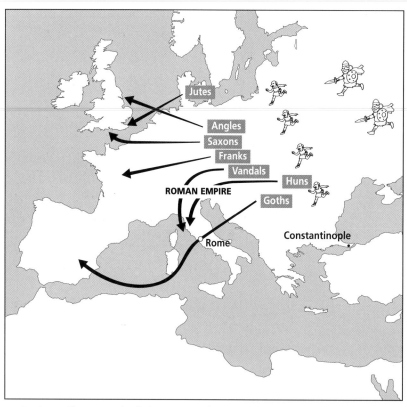

Barbarian tribes attacked the Empire from all directions.

English words which come from Latin words

English	Latin
Navy	*Navis* (a ship)
Video	*Video* (I see)
Science	*Scio* (I know)

Roman numerals are still used today. For example, on clocks.

The Arch of Titus. It was built by the Romans in AD 81.

What have the Romans left us?

Although the Empire came to an end, a lot of Roman things have lived on right up to today.

1 The Latin language

The Romans spoke Latin. Many modern English words come from Latin words (see box).

Coats of arms and badges have Latin sayings on them. Latin is still taught in some of our schools. Flowers and plants all have Latin names.

Source A

2 Books and art

The Romans wrote many plays, stories and poems. They also wrote history books. We still have many of these books.

The Romans were very good at making statues and carvings. Later artists have copied the Roman way of carving statues.

3 The Christian religion

The Romans became Christians. Christianity is still the main religion in countries which used to be in the Roman Empire, such as Britain, Spain, France and Italy.

The Pope still lives in Rome. He is the head of the Roman Catholic Church.

4 Buildings

Many Roman buildings were very grand. They were so well built that some are still standing.

- Much of the Colosseum in Rome is still standing.
- Parts of Hadrian's Wall can still be seen.
- Some Roman roads are still in use. The modern A1 was once a Roman road called Ermine Street. It is a very straight road.

Many later builders copied the Roman way of building (see Source B).

Conclusion

The Romans controlled large parts of Europe, North Africa and the Middle East. It is here that Roman things have been left behind. So in these parts of the world the Romans have not been forgotten.

But we must also remember that millions of other people in the world never saw a Roman. If you go to South America, Japan or Australia you will not see any old Roman buildings.

Source B

The Arc de Triomphe in Paris, built in 1806–36. You can see how the French have copied the Romans.

Questions

1 Read **The end of the Roman Empire**. Why did the Roman Empire end?

2 Look at the numbered sub-headings on these pages. Make a list of things the Romans have left us.

amphitheatre a round unroofed building with rows of seats surrounding an arena.

archaeologists experts who study the remains of ancient civilizations that are buried in the earth.

artefacts everyday objects.

auxiliaries foreign troops used to fight for a country at war.

centuries the smallest band of soldiers in the Roman army consisting of 80–100 men.

chain-mail armour made of metal rings linked together.

cohort a group of six **centuries** (480–600) men, in the Roman army.

drill training in military exercises.

excavation the digging of trenches in the ground to uncover ancient remains.

faeces waste matter from the body.

fortified a place or building strengthened against attack with walls or ditches.

hypocaust under-floor heating system.

Legacy of Rome the Roman influence on life throughout the Empire that remained for centuries: e.g. Roman roads, buildings, language, literature and art.

legate soldier in command of a legion.

legion the largest division of the Roman Army, (5000 men, 10 cohorts).

manoeuvres large-scale exercises of troops.

merchants traders who bought and sold goods with foreign countries.

mineralised changed slowly into a mineral over a long period of time.

mosaics patterns made by placing together small pieces of coloured glass or stone.

province lands in one country ruled by another country.

Renaissance the revival during the 15th and 16th centuries of classical art and learning.

republic a state run by elected representatives of the people.

scabbard a sheath (case) for a sword.

settlement a group of houses like a small village.

slingers soldiers who hurled stones at the enemy with slings.

Specia family gods. Every Roman family worshipped their own household gods who, they believed, would protect them throughout life.

standard flag or carving carried on a long pole by the standard bearer – an important soldier – to inspire the soldiers to follow him into battle.

tenants farmers and workers who rented land or buildings from the owners of country villas.

trident three-pronged spear.

vallum walls and ditches built as a defence.

visor hinged shield attached to a helmet to protect the eyes.

INDEX